A Film in Which
I Play Everyone

Also by Mary Jo Bang

POETRY

Apology for Want

The Downstream Extremity of the Isle of Swans

Louise in Love

The Eye Like a Strange Balloon

Elegy

The Bride of E

The Last Two Seconds

A Doll for Throwing

TRANSLATION

Inferno by Dante Alighieri

Purgatorio by Dante Alighieri

Colonies of Paradise by Matthias Göritz

A Film in Which
I Play Everyone

poems

Mary Jo Bang

Graywolf Press

This publication is made possible, in part, by the voters of Minnesota through a Minnesota State Arts Board Operating Support grant, thanks to a legislative appropriation from the arts and cultural heritage fund. Significant support has also been provided by the McKnight Foundation, the Amazon Literary Partnership, and other generous contributions from foundations, corporations, and individuals. To these organizations and individuals we offer our heartfelt thanks.

Published by Graywolf Press
212 Third Avenue North, Suite 485
Minneapolis, Minnesota 55401

www.graywolfpress.org

Published in the United States of America
Printed in Canada

ISBN 978-1-64445-247-9 (paperback)
ISBN 978-1-64445-248-6 (ebook)

2 4 6 8 9 7 5 3 1
First Graywolf Printing, 2023

Library of Congress Control Number: 2022952327

Cover design: Kyle G. Hunter

Cover art: Dorothea Tanning, *Self-Portrait*, 1944. Oil on canvas; 24" x 30" (60.96 cm x 76.2 cm). San Francisco Museum of Modern Art, Purchase, by exchange, through a fractional gift of Shirley Ross Davis. © 2022 Artists Rights Society (ARS), New York / ADAGP, Paris. Photograph: Katherine Du Tiel.

For Norma Jean

CONTENTS

5

HAMLET.

O God, I could be bounded in a nutshell and count myself a king of infinite space, were it not that I have bad dreams.

—*Hamlet*, act 2, scene 2

A Film in Which
I Play Everyone

FROM ANOTHER APPROACH

The year is still the perpetual now
refusing to escape its frame:
the egg unbroken, the angles as sharp

as ever. The man in the next room
is breathing. The woman, that's me, .
is wondering what we will have

at the end of the day. Wine or water
from a frozen-over lake?
The line between the two blues, water

and sky, you and I, is no longer as fine
as it once was. I want you, the water
would say if water could speak.

Nothing is speaking. This is all
the waiting you could ever want.
Waiting to know if the air will be purer

tomorrow, if the grass will be greener
tomorrow. Will the wildfires burn
themselves out? Will the night scene

with moonlit details go on and on,
as if the personified day
had effaced herself from the calendar

and left us to realize an alternate
destiny: staring at the monsters
who look enough like us to be us—

but for a part of the heart. The small
but necessary part of the heart
that we beg in the middle of the night

to calm us with a quieting chorus of
"There, there, my similar, there, there."

HERE WE ALL ARE WITH DAPHNE

Here we all are at the waterfall, aligned and fixed
like the stars overhead: that limited canopy
under which the laughter of a cosmic joke

echoes out into space. I'm one of the many
waiting for the billow to be
like it is on the sea—full-bodied, beautiful,

a more than adequate distraction
from the war that gets fought inside.
We are all dying but some more than most,

so says my interiority. It talks to me
as green fills the screen. It takes my arm
and walks alongside me. I never ask

where I'm going. I know I'm not meant to arrive.
Me in my nice clothes—cutwork dress,
blindfold of bark from the moment

a man turned me into a tree. "See," he said,
"isn't this all for the better? You with no mouth
to speak of?" By you he meant me.

THE WAR

It begins with a gesture and then grows
into a military tank that begins
to speak in death-speak.

A guard's eye watches
from behind a screen that conceals
his embarrassing thoughts about being.

He goes tramping across whatever continent
he finds in front of him, relishing the metals
and gemstones as if they were canapés

and day was a dance party
and night was a novel set in a feather bed.
Chapter four is for those young enough

to not know what took place
in the garden, those who didn't
have to hide under a hedge, watching

as the Minotaur's feet came closer.
I was told to breathe in/breathe out,
like an iron lung blowing air into an acorn

into which a pinhole had been drilled
on either side. Listen, I was told,
to the death rattle while you pretend

you're underwater in a river of kindness
that loves only you.
You know nothing will get you through this.

A MINIATURE

In my numb mind, a little leather jacket,
the sleeve no bigger than a thumb drive.
In that diminished instance,
I light a cigarette. I put on lipstick.

I'm a version of a self. I speak the truth.
As if speaking French. Haltingly.
Fast-forward and it's me asking air
to save me from the synaptic patterns

that dictate who I am alongside what I do
when under duress. I wear a red dress.
A coral neck scarf. A hand (not mine)
covers my mouth. Nature is never fair.

Someone sucks the air out of the room.
I am saying no more except to say
that the scale is tilted toward
accident. The accidental. The absolute is.

GREEN EARTH

The crush beneath your feet: green grass.
The you-are-here locator. Your eyes
close. You shake your head and think,

the sea was once everything we needed.
Bowie singing, Do you like girls or boys.
Bowie saying, I'll finance the film version

in which I'll play everybody.
The siren gets twinned in the violence
of a scene that refuses to end. This is

the world is a statement. So is: a day will
meet the splintered ends of what went
before it: the inhumanity, the rottenness.

Night rolls in to stand watch, to see
if we find our way. This on a rock moving
through air, a century ticking away.

OUR EVENING IS OVER US

It's the trading in of the workday categories:
hours, clouds that linger inside plate glass
corner windows, a man's head

blocking the view—to become instead
a faint future caption at the bottom
of a photo of hibiscus. There is

no getting around the fact that each of us is
a world of our own. An entity. A pageant
of one. Just like you, I feel my way

forward, letting the back of my hand
brush against the matte wall as I watch
the chiaroscuro movie of my mind.

There should be no anxiety
in knowing the world will die when we die.
This is how it is with us—

the real is wherever we are.
The days refuse to stay put. Speaking is
a way of living with the ruin we were given.

THE KEY

You have to go back to being immature,
a timed regression essential
to running up a further lifetime of debt.

I owe you, the polar bear says,
an icy French OUI. A kiss on both cheeks,
plus a wish to sit on a bench

at the center of a green-painted park,
your legs planted. The unique sensory
effect of the mind holding on to itself

while steadying the sky in order
to sustain the injury and the after-effects
of the earthquake, the cutoff

that occurs against your will
where you have to turn off in order
to engage with the light that comes in

to announce the day's breathing
and being in a complicated network
made of a mesh that allows everything

to fall through. This goes on throughout
the day and night where you dream
of being better than you ever imagined:

a surgeon holding a freehand scalpel—
the cut the metal makes closes on its own
and afterward, everyone walks away well.

HOTEL INCOGNITO

I was here once but not looking like I do now.
Someone filmed me on the balcony.
A man held my hand while dancing. You can see
I was wearing a backless black dress. On the way

out, I ran into a mean girl I'd known years before.
She was basically the same, equally awful
but older. She told me she'd married a judge.
How apt, I thought, how simply beyond repair.

The pavement outside the plate glass sparkled
in lamplight, mica embedded in a mattress
of slate. I was walking away. The ghostly X
at the center of the turning door kept pushing me

out. I was going through the motions of deciding
I didn't belong, not then, not there, not anywhere.

SOME IDENTICAL TWIN SISTER, ONE STEP AHEAD

The day shimmers with silver bouncing off the surface
of a pond-size July—some identical twin sister,
one step ahead, looking back without stopping.
Can time keep capturing an animal
even after it's turned itself in? Cellblock of an instant,
mug shot of an afternoon faun, a disappearance
at the border of a forest, a bed of narrow-gauge needles.
A sparkling pool at the park's edge,
a botanical garden defined by the never-ending echo
of a Deco clock. The ornamental myth of floral love,
carried over moment by moment, repeating
ad infinitum. You point to something: the doll
in the side yard, her plastic teeth perfect in moonlight.
You open your mouth to let the hush in.
You and she dressed alike in visible luminous blue.
When asked, you'll make manifest your ideal smile,
your adaptable funhouse face. Punishment will find you
when a fever fractures into pieces the durable rod
of your long-standing spine. A coat slips
from your shoulders: in its pocket, the magical half tab
you're waiting to take. Rimbaud to Paul Demeny,
in ink, in a folded letter, You have to be a seer to see.
What you really want is to be a camera,
documenting the height you're about to fall from.

THIS IS ME WHEN I WAS BUSY WITH MY NEEDLE

—my back in shadow and my blanket-
wrapped mind buzzing behind my forehead.
My thoughts like the ouroboros
in the *Enigmatic Book of the Netherworld*.

Eyes closed, non-retinal, I see figures
making figure eights on an ice rink,
volcanic lava spilling down the sides
of a mountain, a kettle of vultures circling,

becoming smoke rings imitating
typewriter ribbons. Smoke hovers
in the air like that blown by the caterpillar
in a long-ago story. I see the C

in a gray cat walking on air. See England
and hear myself asking, Why?
When I lived there, I spoke into a silence
so no sound came back.

There was that time when forests meant
bluebirds, rainbow fish, evergreens.
That I can't remember. I think
we sold the farm even though we were told

not to. Who listens to anyone anymore?
The straight pin's a needle, no eye.

FOUR BOXES OF EVERYTHING

1.

In the background, music. In the foreground,
the kind of thinking a mirror appears to do,
giving back the unexpected, depending on
how it's positioned. We thought the world

would change and we would make our own
oval empire out of cameo profiles.
Why you are you and I am I must be
a half thought carved into a crib ornament

that ensures both sides of Apollo will look
down upon us. Freud watches
while we handle the ornament and wonder
about our own otherness—a different form

of separation anxiety where what comes back
is the fact that each of us is alone and standing
in front of a winter garden where, no matter
what time of year, it's winter. We wear green

coats while the camera holds us in its lens.
Only the polestar sees us as we really are.
A bell rings, the gate opens, and out pours
a chorus: "The undiscovered country . . .

puzzles the will, / And makes us rather bear
those ills we have / Than fly to others
that we know not of?" That stained moment
stays and serves us tea. A bent feather sighs

about the air. When the book closes, we open
it again just to see ourselves in the margin.

2.

The camera angle is from above exactly
like the view of an angel looking down
on Earth from the distance
of an archway over a doorway. Such

sadness. Dante embracing Virgil, Milton
holding on to Satan, his daughters
around the table talking well into the night.
What did Charlotte say about Jane?

Whatever, she wore a bi-dyed full-length
blue-green dress with which to say it.
Not a man, she said, not a woman
but an author. That's how you can count

on me to come to you. The film goes soft,
the way the chin of a charm-school scholar
blurs when dusted by her fox-fur collar
each time she makes a single-shoulder

shrug. Dickinson writing, I only meant you
were a flower in an extraordinary garden.
Meaning, she was also something other.

3.

To close the no-go zone. To live with
one's difference. Fanatic is inspired by a god.
Fancy is whim, inclination, desire. Or elegant,
fine, ornamental. Fancy man attested from

eighteen-eleven. A fanfare can be a flourish
of trumpets. Fanny Hill in *Memoirs of a Woman
of Pleasure* (1748). A woman holds a fan.
She picks up her train with her other hand.

The background is bipartite. The dividing line
confirms: if you feel like a misfit, you are one.

4.

On the last day of a year, fireworks in windows.
Pink-and-blue metallic blurring. A barely
decipherable landscape made out of trees
and darkness. In the kitchen, a triptych-mirror

encounter—finally a verifiable trinity. The red
ink of my mind sinks in while my head
registers a train barreling over the edge. Smoke
covers the world, a silver bird ticks. The scene

is the self's displacement from a place where
only dotted lines divide any two things,
one from the other. The concrete sky insists
on rain. The door opens. I reach out my hand,

find a melting-snow heaviness that runs
a fine-tooth comb through the air, transforming
the mist into pale gray haze. Tomorrow
becomes the day I'm waiting for.

I make a mark on the wall for the day. I count
my mistakes. I stand still, staring straight
at the thinking reeds. The bee goes about its way,
sleeping in a state of detachment, then opening

its eyes and seeing calla lilies and caterpillars.
A revved-up snowplow pushes time across
the prairie, a map of furrows and folds. I stay
facing the past, which, in this case, is a box

where a Cupid bow-and-arrow set reminds me
of the archaeologist who dug up a Roman mosaic,
took one look, then covered it over again,
having decided some secrets are better left buried.

A FILM IN WHICH I PLAY EVERYONE

In scene two, silence is a sleeve, I'm an arm in it.
In an outdated *Hollywood* magazine, I found a photo

of someone wearing my hair. How can that be?
Now I can't stop thinking about the synaptic sparks

over which no one has any control. Or, they have some
control but not enough to count on in a crisis.

I'm making sense all the time of all the senseless endings.
A day is as long as the time it takes

for the mind to consider life and death countless times.
Which must make a day plus a night a highway

we're only vaguely aware of since we're busy
sitting in a chair or lying on a bed

with a floral-print bedspread or walking to the store
past someone with a dog on a leash and a phone

in their hand, into which they seem to be saying,
"That is not what I meant blah, blah, blah,"

to an absent ear. Home, you unpack the items
you bought, crease the bags flat, stack them out of sight.

All without saying a word. This is a nonspeaking part.
You're an extra. That day you were filmed

on the steps walking into the school dance,
the costume you wore was pure you.

The set for the scene where everyone disappears
was painted Parisian sky-blue. The air burned

like a curtain on fire. The fire kept going out,
then being relit, a trick candle on a cake made of clouds.

A SET SKETCHED BY LIGHT AND SOUND

Outside, there's barking. The radio's on
loud but no one is talking. The long day
is darkening. Two silver stars are parking
at the curb, a long silent line. Reading

Charles Lamb, on the truth: "They do not
so properly affirm, as annunciate it." Like
an angel, I wondered? Like a Gabriel
telling a girl the facts of life: You spread

your legs and yes, just like that—a sudden
baby crying behind the face of a girl
staring at the treetops outside the clerestory
windows of a church of one. The rain

comes in around the frames, a thin trickle
that makes the concrete go gray. A bell
sounding, fine-tuned to a storm. A bell, or
even better, a siren. An alarm that tells

of the need to absent yourself, to lie down
and behave as if you have no agency,
snug against the wall. The path formed
by the water is a line that holds the brain

hostage as it goes on being one detail,
becoming one more in a body of minutia,
one end ending then—another, years later
in a new now, listening to the outside

come in through the window. Between
time one and time two, a chasm opens:
into that, you sweep the sounds. That,
in turn, turns off the harsh light falling on

the event. The curtain over who you were.
You, as everything that happened to you.
You, that time, being told what to do.

THIS MORNING

This dawn, the light isn't blue
but the deepest charcoal residue
of a forest burned to the ground
before the rain came through.

My face keeps competing
with the gray of an ocean of grief
pressed into ovals. I know
there will be no coming back

from this. It's the same unease
known by anyone caught between
being awake and the spacey state
of having dozed off at the wheel.

The dawn window grows into
the maggot day. The air is dense
in front of the glass and also
as far as anyone has ever seen.

I AM ALREADY THIS FAR

And yet I've still said nothing about the water,
how glassy it was, or the canvas tarp of a tent.
I remember the sound of the hammer
driving the stakes. The anxiety, the smell,

the aftermath of returning and going back
to school and being sent home. Fuck that
back and forth. I cut the pages of a thick book
and put the cigarette pack in the space I'd created.

Then I insulted my sister who went and told
my mother I'd lied. What was I thinking?
If you ask me today, I can tell you. I was trying on
a new self, acting as if I were already me,

following a path, seeing green, stopping to sit
under a tree, lighting a cigarette. A static moment
of looking back at where I'd been and seeing
the past was coming with me. My antennae tuned

to a television in the background, my eyes glued
to a book that kept changing, me breathing
in the translation. There would be the sound
of a train because there always is. It codes

for the day you'll sit next to someone and tell them
your secrets. Then get up again, a new man-
ner of speaking. The made clothes. My own odd
fragility. Even if I could bring her back

I wouldn't. It's better this way. Her in glass and me.

NO QUESTIONS

Blast zone, shock wave, viral progression
until there you are, no longer you
but what you've been made into.
You falling, rising, bobbing, weaving,
and this you that you know so well
can go on for a lifetime. You know all
there is to know about lying down
and about taking it and this is because
you are a woman and this is what
you were taught women do. Shredded,
red heart, lungs, then cell after cell,
like someone walking behind you,
watching to see if you trip. And you will.
If not, they trip you up. It's what they do.

THE THERAPIST

The therapist wears pretty dresses
and I sometimes so want to touch them.
It makes my throat close to think of that fabric
under my fingers. One day, a Wednesday,

I asked, May I? She nodded as if she too knew
that that small act of intimacy would bond us
together for life. And it has. She lives now
inside a synapse where I'll never get rid of her.

One more metal link in the collar
that's unclasped each evening in dreamland
where I pretend I'm a well-behaved blue-
burlap dog walking along beside Anna Freud.

Arf. Arf, arf. The oncoming cars slow
on the curve as we pass. Are they looking
at us? It's not possible to know. This is the way
of the world. Us and them, me and her,

my cells devolving daily into a mash-up
of past and present, with and without.
The instability is dizzying. Ditto the revving
autos and scent of petrol. I form-fit myself

to the air the same way confession-booth
breath conforms to the shape of a closet.
Similarly, my clouded face fades into the foam
pillow when I lie down at night. This is her,

I say. This is me. This is the want I didn't want
when I had it but now, it is all that I have.
A facsimile. A flowering pear tree's off-season
leaves. The July scent of metal being beaten

by a hammer and bouncing up and off
the high-gloss surface of a silver-plated lake.

THE SHORTHAND METHOD

is something like a head shaking no, no, no or shoulders shrugging
maybe. A nod can sometimes stand for yes or, yes, I guess.
That's the confusion that shortening causes. Better to say, Yes,
I am I, and act like you. You might add, I think as I move

through space. Or, ask the question, what is love but a form
of trying to see in low-light conditions? A girl makes a world
that is odd, bent, inverse. She reads and says yes to
"I felt it in every fiber of my being. I was shaken

by what it implied: A stronger god than I is about to take control.
That's exactly when the animal within—which occupies that attic
room where all the sense perceptions travel, especially the visual—
was filled with awe and said to the eyes: Get ready

to see blessedness. Then the primitive part of nature, at the most
basic level of the gut, began to cry and crying said:
Hello misery, my suffering is going to go on forever."
In French, blessed is wounded. Shorthand: I am, therefore sorrow.

THE THEORY OF PERSONALITY

Is change even possible? The color of the sky
can be altered by a blue-dot sugar cube melting

on a tongue. Someone's green glove decapitates
a daisy (deadhead removal of a dead flower

head). The petals gesture: she loved me once,
she is no longer. In some languages, a window

is said to give—as in the window gives onto
a forest or a backyard garden. A pale-yellow

chrysanthemum can stand in for the sun above
the same window but it won't give light.

A fashion craze for leather pants can easily
alter your view of skintight. There is, of course,

that surrealist train, the one that is continually
leaving the station while staying right where it is.

BEFORE THE ABSOLUTE PERFECTION DYING ACHIEVES

is the potential for memory to err. Stop me,
the mouth says to the mind, as the dashboard
races to a waiting disaster. Which is exactly

like saying stop to water in a cup in the midst
of overturning. Holy water snakes its way
down the forehead, a motion devised

to mirror our anxieties about being good
enough. A catechism arranges the negatives
in a circle: my grimy childhood, my nervous-

making standing on the edge of the canyon,
my body tilting toward emptiness below. My
early Bethlehemic lumbering. Before we reach

the abyss, time flips from I-didn't-know then
to what-I-know now. The breeze hushing
the birds sends messages to anyone

listening in on the scattershot hail
on the windowpane. I am examining the sill
as an unbroken line dividing outside from in,

knowing that that border also marks the point
when living is over. The hour of lead.
Imagine it. Could you move? Now you think.

REIGN OF TERROR

You've been here before
and never again, the mantra repeats
its sick drumbeat.

The door like an upstanding stick
waiting to be kicked
in or down or around.

Kicked around.
That's as close as it gets.
Instability can't be forced to stand still.

Neither can static.
You can't hear yourself
over the sound of the manic drum.

Over the slice
of the guillotine knife
bringing home its bucket of blood.

THE CROWD CLOSES IN

Above the crowd closing in were the three stars
that stood for three men, plus the constellation
of the girl with her legs apart, delivering one
nebula and the well-named Pillars of Creation.

Rain was now bringing light to the clouds
across an expanse, while I continued on my way
to the scaffold. I had erred. Of course,
there were others before me. There was

Kafka and the problem of the father. Electra
and the problem of the mother. Freud
and the problem of the he, she, or they,
one kept wanting to see through the keyhole.

There was green, and all that green means,
including the neon highway to heaven.
There was C, whom I truly did love once,
and S, whom you could say I still did.

As soon as I said it, I knew I was wrong.
When the trapdoor below me opened, I froze
in terror. This after having navigated the way
back from the border known as the brink.

THE WALLPAPER BEHIND THE DAY

Calm down, I tell myself.
Come down to earth-based science.
The random at-rest fire that chars
the inside of the braincase gray. The

impossible heat that pours forth from
the atmospheric furnace of despair.
I tell myself, this forged metal cylinder
of atoms and molecules, nerve endings

and sand-grain coral generators,
is not out to get you. The harmless
electrical farcical repetition
of the do-nothing sparks from the gun

that solders it all together, and which
is what thinking is, keeps on nonstop
and makes a mess of the toy-store
dream of a ball that rolls down

a timeless hill to reach a blue-green
sea and float there for a small eternity
in a chasm. Hades, in order
for anyone to die, must be released.

Hades says to someone, "Please, let me."

ELEGY FOR TWO

If I could bring back two,
it would be you and you.
One summer. One winter.
One dresser. One dress,

sleeveless in any season.
One day wiped from the face
of the white-leather moon
at the moment of waking.

The bed below it, empty,
as it was before you were.
Night shuts the door
of the train as it leaves

the station again and again.
I'm sitting next to you.
The three of us are now,
on our way to nowhere new.

THE DEAD OF WINTER

The cold is a knife-slice on the skin.
The mind says no, over and over.
This is not what you want.

What you want is that crimson
cover called love: the pulsing
blood-rush that provokes

a small metamorphosis. An object,
held by a gaze, radiating being.
You would say passion but a demon

has sewn your lips shut. The silver
needle lies there like the melting
sunlit snow beneath your feet.

It looks up as if to ask, Tell me, how
often do you feel the way you feel?

THE ECHO

for Lucie Brock-Broido

The transient snow in a shaken globe was making me think
of the Moscovian dome, below which,
in a small private room called a cubiculum, I'd read

they had buried an empress's golden hair.
After she'd died, after "they inquired eagerly
for the tsarina, but she was nowhere to be found."—

From the Remotest Periods to the Present Time.
Snow becomes rain under the overhead rainforest
showerhead—drop by imbecilic drop dripping

onto a broken stone floor. About the absolute fracture
that death represents, my brain believes in what I believe:
like any animal, we make our way. Amphibian. Reptilian.

Mammalian. Some days more than others, I put away one
moment and up comes another, a replenishing
gold Virgilian bough. Outside, snow engulfs the asphalt,

the sidewalks, the drivers. In a second, it seems
a million trains enter and exit the tunnel.
The flood-protective walls rise, a tower of torn eaves

over a storm-drenched oubliette. The dome dissolves,
leaving only the ineffable portion of this time and the idea
that we who are still here have kept what was left of her.

HANGING THE CURTAIN

The curtain was meant to hide the zoo
of my petty vices, but instead
it was a coat that kept falling off
my shoulders, revealing a watch

that kept adding up the hours.
After finishing my shift, I sat with a pill
in my hand, then thought better of it
and dropped it back into its plastic.

In the family album, I stood at the edge,
a dented girl with a divided mind.
Daily, the same awareness: it was only
a matter of time before someone

would act with cruelty. Now, looking back,
I see "Will you, won't you join the dance?"
as the ever-pestering question.
In the side yard, six rabbits in a cage,

lettuce torn to bits. Silent rats consorting
with rusting tin cans at the bottom
of the drainage ditch—occasional victims
of a stepfather's shotgun. Once

a year, fireworks sounded the night out.
A weeping shrub occupied the corner yard,
the flowering branches bent like water
falling from an active fountain.

When I hit my limit, I crawled under it
to escape the conceptual blur.

AWAKE, I LISTENED

to the broken sound of a puppet's voice
that caused the air to fix itself into a dense curtain
that couldn't be seen through. I heard the puppet say,

"You're going nowhere." It knew cruelty
when it saw it: rain, snow, ice hanging off eaves,
cages, knives, cudgels, the slap across its puppet face.

At the same time, a tight spring was coming undone
beneath a hand holding it down. It was the self
that lived under lock and key in the netherworld

of morning, noon, and night. That's when
I saw I would never know enough to keep a moment
in its track and my eyes on the devil I didn't want

to believe in but now found it impossible not to.

EYES OPEN, I PROCESS THE DATA

Eyes open, I process the data and in time
become aware of the way it all works: the corruption

that causes the synaptic activity to become a coat
of metal I walk around wearing.

Night is a blanket over barking dogs.
The new girl has a paperback with two girls on the cover.

I pick it up and ask, "Why?" "Why not?" she answers.
Dear God that doesn't exist, we are identical—

or soon will be. I evoke you, I leave. And just so,
you are gone. A few tears shed on the way there and back.

The tow-rope up the mountain, the fast-track down.
I take the landscape with me. I stood looking backward:

the white whale was standing upright on its tail.
At that point, I had no fight in me.

The Spain trip snapshots came back blurred:
the bob haircut, the chair wearing a pale pink slipcover,

the painted lips of a red goldfish, the frayed ribbon
bordering the Freudian curtain above an infantile crib.

An idea arranges itself in the cerebellar parenchyma:
to rend or to rip is to tear off into tiers.

THE FABLE OF A FABRIC WOVEN WITH RESISTANCE

One way to see it is: the self is infinite
and circular, like problematic thoughts
about how mice bred for insomnia
fall into a deep-dish sleep, but wake
not long after. Those thoughts
get mixed in with a treasure trove
of purple lilacs beside a door,
a porcelain sink slick with water
from a tap, like snow-melt from ice,
and a NO heard outside the circle
of the skull that keeps repeating
ad infinitum while inside the brain
an insect enters and hums all night.
In the morning, it finally exits,
like an insect will when it wants to
hide from a noise that won't stop
telling it, "Do this or else"—and when
it resists, takes a fat thumb and presses
down until being is nothing but a body.

SOMETIMES I COME TO AND WONDER

To be forever inside the revolving universe
has never been my dream and yet
while I was here, I wanted knowledge.

I knew I could see inside myself
but no one else could. I had no second self.
And if I had? Escape is what one does

for an interval before returning to a town
square where someone with a fractured leg
is lying, a mistreated dog is being eyed

by an indifferent crowd, a rotting scrap
of meat is being eaten while a worker waves
a palm-frond just to keep the flies off

once the maggots hatch. How to make sense
of that? Thank you, Dr. Freud. Flawed yes,
and yet. Ahead, I see a gate opening. I go in.

WHAT I'M COVERING OVER

is the seething beginning
where I saw things but didn't know
what they meant.

The touching world
kept putting its hands on me.
There is no way to replicate

what made no sense
when it happened. What anything
might mean after the fact

is simply conjecture. That said, I am
still alive inside it and so see it
acting like a glass tumbler code

where the usual method is: one
number turns while the others wait,
then the next, the next, the next—

not in the same row but all eventually
and, rarely but sometimes, all
turning at once. Sitting here now,

the chasm below is the dizzying
Grand Canyon all over again, and
sadly, all over the world.

The expansive NOW with its glowing
circle moves into place like a globe
one can't actually know

because it's always changing.
Whole countries come and go.
A secret retreats into its shell.

I only know what I knew and that
was firsthand. Its little to nothing
keeps me here and makes me think

I would know what hell was
if there were one outside of this one.
Meanwhile, here comes a monster.

TO SAY PLEASE AND YET NOT PLEASE

I ask to be taken away and I'm taken
into a palace where inside is outside
and pure repercussions—where I won't

need I any longer. The towering walls—
ashen, ditto the ceiling but darker.
A blasphemous secular song

spins in surround sound: a woman
is being taken down for refusing
the fealty due to a ludicrous fiefdom.

Bad is about to be worse. The chorus,
hovering above in a saucer,
sings "Assume nothing." I do

as I'm directed and enact. The scene
can be taken for granted—I, a Lady
Jane Grey, am being told to close my eyes,

shut my mouth. The mouth in my head.
The head my mouth will soon be missing.

EVERYTHING THAT WAS IS NOW OWNED

and shared by the clowns: Yes,
they say, to one another, our purses are full
and we are even more content than before.

Overhearing what they say, the lion
finds itself wishing the cosmic pistol
would finally fire and signal the razor

to begin to dig in like a good dog.
The smooth face, both sides, would then
no longer be the fine brush it was.

What had been would now be over
the moon, i.e., on the side that seems
to receive no light. The lion lies down.

The night obscures its losses. The lion has
a thought, I might be able to live like this
but a battered animal is only certain

of the air entering and exiting its lungs
and its face looking down at the nothing
that's left where something once was.

IN THIS ONE WORLD

The grassland comes up to the edge
of the road on which I'm standing.
The car has turned off.

Has been turned off.
A gunshot is easily heard.
The grassland exists. My eyes see

that the land is a banner
the wind holds up. The ground turns
under and around and then becomes

a densely forested park where
the trees are all lying on their sides.
After the hurricane came through,

I couldn't find my way out.
The erasable beginning
kept coming back like a weaving

I took out at night. By noon,
it was yesterday again—a sketch
barely held together by a stitch

or two. As another woman once said,
"A circle lower than this one
is waiting for the one

who kept coming at me."
She knew how nice
a tormenter looks when buried in ice.

WHEN I WAS AN INANIMATE OBJECT

I was dressed in wool and waiting for winter
to leave me alone. Behind me, a table
with an edge where someone had once

permitted a lit cigarette to make a striated mark,
perhaps on a day like this one—cold, wet
and gray in the worst sort of way,

which is when the inside and outside stop
making distinctions. I was not the self I knew
from before. Only the clock behaved,

stopping when I fell over into sleep, starting
when I made my way out. With the door closed,
the city was reduced to the even sweep

of a filtered breeze. The only thing that broke
the silence was a sound that can't be made
audible outside the brain. All day, I sat with that

and with water in a glass. The water
would sometimes send light at an angle
that would briefly illuminate my lightless mind.

THE EXPERIENCE OF BEING OUTSIDE

An insight examined a lifetime
while an ocean flowed under my feet. My feet
no longer felt since my body was beside itself.

I was at an altar, asking the best gods
of the boggled mind to save me,
tossing two more mother-may-I's

into the emptiness. Who would be blamed,
I wondered, for living the life that was mine?
There was no one to ask what it was like

being dead. I imagined a switch
getting tripped as a sheet-glass window gave
permission for each imperfect person to merge

their multiplex selves into one.
A blue bowl caught whatever came next:
birds, clouds, high-wire act reactions.

Whatever you were, you were now altogether
yourself, and happily one with the world.

STAYING IS A FORM OF HAUNTING

Staying is a form of haunting wherever you are,
like the boy in "The Dead" who remains

where he is as he turns into snow.
Slowly things get done. Or done to you.

A miscellany has no end but is only
an encyclopedia with extra blank pages

where endless wishes wait to be recorded.
Sorrow wheelbarrows over a snake and a boat

goes by. I love you, I wanted to say
to the girl, but silence kept sounding

its silver bell. One day, the consumptive blush
of my cheek will flower at the very moment

a red feather blows by, making a perfect match.
She who once loved being me says,

"It's difficult to believe now
that you once wanted to belong to never."

FAR FROM HERE

Far from here, in an astrophysical wormhole
that spanned an infinite distance, there the triple
goddess had three of everything: faces, throats,
voices, etcetera, etcetera, etcetera—all irrefutable
evidence that tripling and the trinity existed long before

the triad of furies was unleashed on Prometheus once
he'd been made very "fast by tying with fetters and
chains." Along the way, ashen light fell over forests
outside the gaping mouths of caves. Power
got concentrated in the hands of a conquering few

who swept aside freedom and invented a female avatar
for every anxious damning force that falls like water
on us. A cat now played with a snake in lieu of a mouse.
The rabbit in the moon stood like a raven
on a writing desk while priestly Adam looked down

at a birdbath at the middle of the orchard. He saw
only his own face in the water and therefore
insisted the rabbit was a man. Cain was thinking.
Abel was absent. Lilith was threatening to leave.
The moon was on her side. Full circle means you keep

coming back to the beginning again—a snake or else
some stand-in mean queen offering a pretty girl
a poison apple. You overhear an argument that ends
with JUST STOP IT. You might think that has little
to do with this story but that would be far from the truth.

THE ASSUMPTION

The artist Marsden Hartley supposedly said,
"I love falling water—no lake or pond
can give me what a waterfall can."

Can't that go without being said? Or if said,
not quoted as if it were a secret whispered
on a death bed. The upheaval

of a falling wall of water has more drama
than a duck pond or a monochrome Lake
Erie? What I'd like to know is how to be

that dramatic. How to let my blue dress
meet the fire coming closer and yet
not burn up completely. My blue dress

or wool scarf or red sweater. Or my skin
melting into the heat of a last day on earth.
Even now, I'm aware of the air stirring

the trees, the bees becoming a shimmering
living satin fabric. A few separating off.
Their terrible stings. The bandaged after.

TODAY YOU'RE THE STILL PHOTOGRAPHER

on a movie set and you see the doctor
who appears to have been hired
to provide first aid for any cut or scrape
an actor might meet with. You know
he's a doctor not by a white coat,
stethoscope, or head-mirror reflector
on his forehead, but because earlier
you overheard somebody ask,
"Who's that?" At "that," the person
to whom the question was addressed
had turned and said, "He's the on-set
doctor." You too had looked
in the direction the first was looking.
You'd noticed the doctor was handsome
and as soon as you did, you'd sensed
you had seen him before.
The feeling wasn't pleasant.
You could even say it was painful. A pain
the size of a toy dog left on a rowboat
adrift in a mist. You saw through the fog
and remembered a moment when
you were very young and a doctor said
you should imagine pain as a number
between one and ten. You now wonder
how he knew you could count.
With the question of counting,
you recall a rhyme: One for sorrow, /
Two for joy, / Three for a girl, /
Four for a boy, / Five for silver, /
Six for gold, / Seven, for a secret
you never told. The director yells, *Cut!*
You didn't know the filming had begun.

THINK OF JANE AND THE REGENCY ERA

It was a very green world. Trees and their leaves,
seven sylvan elves in the depths of the forest,
the rest was left to the imagination. Turn right

here and you'll see how the sea keeps beating up
the boardwalk, lessening it little by little,
like the teacher's disappearing ruler she keeps

up her sleeve. The French lieutenant
is shipping out, leaving the lady who could walk
only two ways, back and forth or up and down.

She stood at the top of the stairs and said,
"By daybreak, I'll belong to whatever's bent
over me." Think of her as both a miss and as

being caught in a misunderstanding. For myself,
I sit down and say, "Don't leave me," to the sky.
"Can you fix me?" I ask the mask in the mirror.

Like the princeling, I ask and ask but no one
brings anything, only a four o'clock miniature
natural-wood table that shape-shifts

into an overturned almond on which one can
take tea and dance if one likes. Inside the story,
men in top hats and a woman with a Juliet cap.

That hat attracts me. As does the woman.
But not everything is possible.
You are only the heroine in your own story.

LIKE SOMEONE ASLEEP IN A CINEMA

Like someone asleep in a cinema who wakes to lean over
into your space and mock your open-eyed wonder.

That's how it was then, the eye movements of others
tracking my every reaction on the stage that ends

by design sans everything. When everything is over,
the shape of the moon will still feign an underworld bathtub

boat, at rest on its side. I'll be the one I've always been,
held by a woman wearing a hat, half veil, half-opened lips,

the whites of her eyes matching the moon as the sun reflects
off its surface. The pockmark above my right eyebrow

will also match. I so wanted to be rock but never achieved it.
Wanted to lie to get what I wanted, without wondering,

What will happen if I lie? My face still stings from the hand
that slapped it. My teeth taste of Fels-Naptha soap. Every act

is literalized. The clock no longer flips number to number,
time keeps making a hissing *is*. Lying is now in fashion.

Lie down with me, people say, when they hold someone back
from the edge of that insane remembering. Floating out

of the mouth is the suds of tomorrow. I will never be clean,
not as long as I live. We watch unrealizable shadows and

make something of them—an eye watching the lashes fall.

CAMERA LUCIDA

Barthes appears to over-read the social
aspects of photographs while
under-reading the formal elements.

In the photograph of Queen Victoria,
he claims there's poignancy in the lesser
social role of the horseman but he says

nothing of how the center oval of bright
light, against which the queen
and the horseman are set, becomes an egg

in which the two incubate. He says
nothing of the way both legs of the horse
and the legs of the standing man disappear

into the unlit border or how the curved line
of the horse's belly, the barrel, matches
exactly an arc formed by the draped edge

of the queen's capacious skirt.
The curved line made by the hem is echoed
in the horse's dock, its breast, the swell

of its cheek, and the U-shape made
by its muzzle. The queen's skirt obscures
any potential phallic evidence

of the horse's maleness, so makes the horse
a mirror of her majesty, the queen.
What else does queen mean except

the feminine sum of unfettered curves?
The horseman is all angles—bent arms,
pleated kilt, peaked collar, flat hat. With or

without a horse, the queen is not him. And
he is not her. That's where the sadness lies.

THIS IS WHAT YOU ARE, THE SELF SAYS TO THE SELF

—a spectrum, an immeasurable gradient, during and after which
the places where you were can be tracked over a sprawling landscape

but to what end? It's always a vast sea of ketamine green,
lace at the top of the breakers. Sediment sinking in. Sleep, eat,
sleep, Sunday touching. Combing through the button tin

to find the pale Lucite disc pierced by two perfect holes.
A fading cardstock movie-popcorn box. The skating-skirt's pink satin
lining now living in a synapse. Later, an ice storm, and later yet,

lake water that was as close to silk as you can get. The snow
breaking into the perfect shape of a boot. Then lying
on a new-made bed. The radiator noise getting louder and louder

like a larval thought fattening, bumping against the braincase
again and again. The girlfriend who lied. Who never let you
touch her back. Play-acting is only one way to say what you want.

There are numerous other methods. Not a spectrum. Not a gradient.
But a constant complication. Desire ever-watchful, an insomniac eye.

A STARTING POINT

I told myself five hundred would be enough
to begin to make a plan. In the end,
it was over two thousand when we divided the cash

we'd kept in a tin. Waiting for him to leave,
I moved seamlessly between assuming
some mindless zen and reading a novel.

He mimed playing a piano, a hyper-emotive
Rachmaninoff, frenetic fingers pressing,
time and again, against the blond laminate

of the kitchen table. He said I would never
be as good as he was. He said it without saying it,
making it clear he was a titan of the industry

of succeeding at being. If anything, I was ancillary
evidence of his genius. The bitterness
of the sneering *Good luck* when he left. I was

stunned. Humiliated. Sick with the sense
of precariousness. And yet, embarrassed to be
thinking of finances. Only now do I see inside

my mind. Unnerved by my own uncertainty,
thinking was hovering above the hot water I was in.
I, a piece of cardboard, feeling my fiber lessening.

The novel was a translation of Stendhal's *The Red
and the Black*. Published in 1830, I read it
as if it were a timeless allegory: the chronic inner

problem of an inescapable provincial beginning.
A social order that would not expand
enough to let an outsider in. Fine, I said. But no. No.

NOTHING COMPARES TO DAPHNE IN GREEN

The quick lens shifts to a fragmenting figure,
then, a new reality: the view over an orchestra
and its shell, a hyper-magnified gray-turning-green,

purl-and-knit-stitch acrylic. The lush texture
silences a thundering bomb blast. I am
now myself and one of several sleepers in a room.

Venus blushes in a window. A knife draws a line
between heaven and earth. The fabric spreads—
one bed becomes a polar landscape, another

an uncut chenille. I think, I might like a carpet—
a carpet or a cat. Each would catch the light
differently. Morning, my face in a basin lake,

I dread fixing my eye on his baffling audacity.
The scene moves like a model Milky Way, entire
and hardly at all. For a moment, the city of sorrow

briefly flips open to the opium eater's *Confessions*.
The mirror tells me I'm the last-act Ophelia
watching the sky go by ("a Cerulean sky. *&c. &c.*")

drowned, but not yet dead, awake and aware.
Over me, droplets melt, drip, and refreeze,
making the multilayered clouds appear to be static.

What remains fragment is the won't-take-no Apollo.
His tepid red-lettuce heart, his wormy vermicelli.

THE PROBLEM OF THE PRESENT

It was like a whip, the animated snapping
of the man lying like an overturned turtle
on the bed in the upstairs bedroom,
his henchmen and henchwomen downstairs,

gliding in the corridors, the new warmth
of the sun in the window reducing itself
to the size of a stamp on the wooden desk
in the empty office. The question is not

whether we have free will, but what choices
history offers us. The strongest force
is conformity, not passion, not even greed
for possessions because who would ever

want a diamond unless they were told to.
Here, someone must have said, you want *this*.

ON THE FACTORY FLOOR

When I first heard fate saying how poor I would be,
I had wanted to ask, "How far will that get me?"
I was sewing a seam that indicated time was worth nothing

much. At the machine, my brain kept melting in at the edge.
The clock was wrapped in cloth. When I paused,
the machine became a crowd encased in ice, waiting to thaw.

The factory buzzed at four, followed by the jolt of an alarm
at the perimeter. Green leopards entered, barely visible
against the gray-green background. I called them

my dollar bills. I kept my fingers crossed and nails cut
to the quick. I was first assigned pieces. When those
became fewer and farther between, I practiced answers

to inane questions: Yes, I left early. Yes, I tried my best. Yes,
the weight of exhaustion sent me to bed. Yes, I'd been told
I was a test case. Yes, I was an example of what not to do

with what I don't know. Each day began with a slight
oscillation while ON switched into action—then, the bimodal
fevered bland. I held on to what little motion there was.

It kept me from toppling over and into the through-hole.
Habit flattened the stairwell, a floor rose up to meet my face
and feet, forming a level plane. The machine's incessant

needle mimed in and out. For me it was like fucking air.

I RAISED MY WRIST TO MY FACE

and watched as one hand quickly closed the interval
while the other, which had fallen behind,
seemed not to move. I thought, What a big stupid

O, that oculus. It only followed that a snake,
unable to find its way out, would swallow its tail
and pretend to be Other. Then keeping time would

begin, then the perpetual story where the second
in line was a girl who got blamed for nature.
Then the stupid wheel, the stupid pinion,

the stupid sluice, the stupid floodgate, the stupid oar,
the stupid mouth dripping spit, and women
sliding under water. Even now, gold is collected

in the front office while in the back men grunt
and rub their origins as a priest with a money belt
whisks in from the hallway to say, "Hey, give us a kiss."

I saw the comic come on and quiet the audience.
I heard her say, "The fool's job is to make the tragic
seem laughable." "Now take your medicine," she said.

THE BREAD, THE BUTTER,
THE ORANGE MARMALADE

Nothing was what I wanted. The bread, white
chalk. The butter, rancidity. The marmalade,
bitterness. The nail on my right hand, the ragged
ending to a difficult day. He'd said, Oh, really,

you're wearing that? I was, I said. But now
there was no room for me in the room.
The lights were too bright. Always a problem
when windows faced the sun. Especially

when the sky showed its face for too long.
No rain for days, then suddenly, rain. I'd worn
the red shoes and now they would be ruined.
How to care less. That phrase, "I couldn't

care less," as if zero were already a viewpoint.
There were two doors into the house: the front
door, which was rarely used, and the side door,
which was accessed by entering the screened

porch where my stepfather's wood was stacked
against the wall. A tall bin of nails anchored
the corner. What was he building now?
The baby was heavy in my arms. If I put him

down, he'd undoubtedly wake. I could tell, time
was a migraine heading straight for my right eye.
The waking baby's cry would be an expert knife
through injured flesh. It was that kind of a season.

CHILDREN WERE ERASING THEIR FACES

So it seemed, as they ran through the room.
Let me know, the man said,
if I begin to play the part of a metronome.

His empty glass was nothing more
than a stem in his hand. She was staring
at the glazed window above his head.

An overactive hand kept opening
and closing it, depending on whether
the sky looked like rain. One long-ago

summer, when the Ozarks had flooded,
toxic masculinity told her stepfather
it was safe to drive across water.

He listened and did it. The water poured in
around the car doors, soaking her feet.
She lived to see him buried in cinders.

The man's glass had somehow filled
itself. Still staring at the window,
she was surprised to see the moon drift in,

as if on a pillow. She'd seen the same thing
in another place but there,
the background sound had been a tractor

skirting a green rectangle. Here, there was
only the din of adult conversation mixed in
with children's high-pitched laughter.

Behind the cloud, an empire of trouble
was sending sparks of Saint Elmo's fire
off the top of a patio lamppost.

Suddenly, a sharp sound. Maybe a starter
pistol setting off a night race across the lake.
That was how she remembered it. It was not,

however, how it happened. Instead,
she had stood at a rail and watched waves
sent back by a cat slapping the water.

A lightning strike lit the sky and revealed
the predicament of a body refusing to give in.
The moon was totally indifferent.

HOW WILL IT FEEL MONTHS FROM NOW

when the pink sliver of sky swims in
through the window and you hear
the high notes from the opera singer
one story below? Angel of wishing,

angel of fortune, the cart overturned,
the small animals from the back
of the truck flooding the highway.
The keys keep making the piano be.

I have only ever wanted the red sky
to turn blue. It's so beautiful
when it sinks in. Hold me, closeness
says. As long as I have sight, I'll see.

The walls of time dissolve whenever
the lights are turned off. The lights
that made the day so easy to be with.
I fold myself away. No mirage

of sirens hammering the glass front
of the hospital down the block.
Stars guide the eye across the sky.
It will be like that. Again, and again.

IN THE MOVIE OF MY UNRAVELING MIND

The forest opens wide then closes once
I'm inside and looking up.

Blue traces the tree line's nothing
above it. The question—Is the sky really

that color?—comes crashing in as it did
on a ledge below which a lake made

figure eights around rocks as I sat
next to someone who said I was not

his original idea of beauty but something.
Something he couldn't quite

put his hands on. Bare neck, shoulders,
legs, all static, all waiting for action

to be taken, as in rehearsing for a play
that opens with a weapon at rest

on the mantel. The gun represents
the fact that whatever's on stage

must be used by the end of act three,
scene something. And yet, there we were.

Neither of us would ever see the other
again except in that film that never ends.

PART OF A LARGER PICTURE

Inside the house, the legs of the bed still hold the scream
that once woke my mother. Mother's soothing
torso can still be seen in the rubber bag on the back

of the bathroom door. Mrs. Dalloway wants flowers.
Andy Warhol wants the flowers to be large and flat
and wants one to be radically different from the others.

There was the room and also what happened in it.
A weight kept being set on top of the base of being.
The space beneath the bed held nothing but air.

The terrible secret self stayed where she was, behind
the curtains. Lashed by an onslaught of echoes,
rain slid down the window while a televised woman

dissolved into the acetate tears of a flickering film.
Mother died, then father. Brother quickly came to be
dead to me. Sister lives on the opposite side of

a see-through resin door. She occasionally waves
me over. Once inside, I speak to myself. And of another.

THE DOCTOR'S MONSTER IS DROWNING

A cameo radio telescope relentlessly pivots
to record the cosmic energy
continually drifting in from the spiral
maze of outer space. It's a mirror of a mirror—

"the core and substance of it untouched."
That agitated turbulence matches
the bizarre distortion of the light that paints
the face and fills the O. Impartial lightning

strikes the water, then disappears. Electricity.
Like Virgil says, each is pulled toward
one's own idea of pleasure. The mind goes on
arguing. "The watch-dogs bark! Bow-wow!"

I close my eyes while forward-facing the lake
until I stop, lie down, and look up to examine
the pattern the light leaves. Ophelia,
I think, looking like she's in a state of thinking

she had never seen anything like it, however,
she had. She drowned. I am as she was
when alive and touching the seam where water
laps over its own edge above and below.

MISTRESS MARY, QUITE

Mary, Mary Quite Contrary, Maxfield Parrish, 1921

Contrary equals: as in realism, also in artifice.
Both act like the diamond-point engraving

done by air, wind, and water in the interest
of accuracy. In the interest of demonstrating

technique to the diamond trade between earth
and the sky where the stars are.

Where the moon is. Where a porcelain nun
behind a wrought iron gate says, "You can't

begin to understand," to a visitor in a hat
who asks, "What's it like in there?" This Mary

that wears gloves, and dresses in dresses, is
sister to the one that is asleep on the job

of resisting the sweep of time that refuses
to let go of what came before. "Mary, Mary,"

someone says. Mary thinks it's her mother
but how can that be when her mother left earth

such a long time ago? She still thinks of her.
She's not that contrary, she has a subjectivity.

THE TRIP

Before the visuals kick in,
there's an ancillary phase, a quasi-auditory
interior ticking so precise it seems mechanistic.

It's a sign that says you're about to be
face-to-face with some bright idea *deus ex machina*
device that drops in solely to contribute

a way out—all in the service of
being extricated from the boxed-in catastrophe
that is your life. You'll be the same you

you were but moved over there, where there is
no more boredom insisting you ignore
the most pleasant fantasy imaginable.

The fact that the trip can't last
will later make the illusion seem cruel. And yet,
you take it. Who wouldn't choose that

over this? Such flawless thinking, you think,
just as thinking reaches its dwindling end.
O happy day, now is now and inside your ever-

obliging mind, you find yourself on
the fluttering edge of oblivion. The longed-for
utopia. The tacit rapture. Tzion. Nirvana.

The heaven that makes you up. The souvenir
photo shows you as you've never seen yourself.

FROM THE EDGE

I'm falling not into a half realization but instead
from the silver rim of the O into the freezing
absolute zero, a concept of no-colder-than
but also the nothing that comes from nothing,
meaning this is what happens when you let go

of a debt. The needle in the arm, the quiet
becoming a steady quick tick-tick-tick, the steep
drop into the eddy-center, followed by
a skittering brain-race across a lake to a place
where Astro Lantern lava lamps fill the windows

of a mutable cityscape stage set that is nothing
but a parallel plane where the aerial dead come to
say hello: he, she, they, daughter, son. Sometimes
you think you would like to die like this rather than
go on and on like a herd animal roaming goes.

WHAT WOULD I HAVE BEEN

What would I have been without the love of ritual?
The little given, the lot taken, a mother in name.
The green afterglow of the eaten globe.
This love of redoing, the dazzling trust game,

arms fallen into over and over. What would I have
been without leaving one realm for another
where quiet was better below the lined walkway.
I walk, a none in a mask of one, obedient to the day's

seven-tab history of search and search for what is
never centered not now and not then. And now this:
to have known what I know and to have done all
that I did, and be about to leave again and again, I

grow thinner and thinner, disappearing
ad infinitum into what must be done to keep being.

I COULD HAVE BEEN BETTER

if I hadn't been me but I was stuck
with my head tracking my thoughts,
my self tracing each second back
to a biblical beginning where

A was A and Eve was some elusive
bog-buried Lucy deep in the silt
of a mythic mountain where
Sisyphus opened his red leather diary

and copied down the same daily
assignment. Once, in the middle
of a disaster, a procedural
policewoman knocked at my door

to ask whether I was all right.
Yes, I said, I was, but only if
we discount the present.
Later, lying in the bed I was born in,

I tallied my many errors, then added
my everlasting love of the few
I'd caught sight of in the midst
of being me. It was as if I had gone

to another country and now
couldn't return without leaving part
of myself behind. I wanted to say
I love you but each time I tried,

the past tense pushed through.
There at the edge of the water—
Venus was where I'd last left her,
standing on a half shell, staring hard

at reeds bending in the wind. She & I
both wanted to see something change.

ON THE NATURE OF HARDWIRING

It used to be I thought all the boats on the horizon
were defined by what was going on inside

the boats and, therefore, meant nothing to me,
standing on land. Now I see that regardless

of perspective, the waves pass like the ultra-slow
beats of a brain engaged in the task of humming along.

The oxygen-enriched blood adds up the signals sent
on the cellular level and creates an undeniable sense

of being. The change in my own thinking
can be traced back to the day a lesson got fixed

in my excitable synapses. Afterward, everything I did
became a trajectory. I thought I would go on

and thinking made it possible. Which surprised me.
I'd found a way to go to the bottom of the world,

see the earth without me, then come back up changed.
Science itself, I could see, knew my altered perception

must be accurate because I read, in print,
that when a mouse was "put under" "the ultra-slow

waves persisted" "but with the direction . . . reversed."
Which I took to mean, even unconscious, one continues.

I WAS DREAMING

a gigantic Federal-style marble bank
building with one long hall
hung with portraits, behind which,
a locked storeroom filled with
stacked cans of paint. I counted twelve
knickknacks on the bank president's desk.
Four children in frames. I can see that
the dream is acting like a movie camera.
While I watch, a former lover succumbs
to being what Barthes calls a "whatever
anything." She resents this. She wants
to be a well-developed thought. It's clear
to me now that she is nothing more
than a scaffold. I urge her to distinguish
herself. Develop an obsession, I say.
I hand her a sincere little boy who keeps
begging her to behave. I tell them both
that only if they wake will they be capable
of changing. The boy explains
that he and the woman are a single
dream trope for doubling. I say no,
they are meant to illustrate the differences
between any two objects,
no matter how similar they seem.
Even so, the boy says, there are similarities.
Even so, I say, there are limitations.

THE ACTUAL OCCURRENCES

The actual occurrences—death and New York
and all the other discernable elements
that made up the inevitable present—

were responsible for defining who I was
at any given moment. The result was
some curated notion of now that appeared

as hazy as a fogged-up window
keeping its eye on a winter blizzard. Still,
there was the sense of a matter-of-factness

that at times even had a quasi-scientific
presence, similar to a magnified photograph
of a distant quasar. That was something

I could hold on to. This is real, I would say
when trying to tease apart what was
inside my mind and what was happening

outside. I treated anything I could see,
no matter how transient, as if it were
a treasured possession, a gift from a friend

who practiced time-space travel—always
forgetting what life was like on earth—
and then whenever she wanted a bit

of attention, came back, barged in
and carried on about having been ignored.
You weren't even here, I told her.

ONE COULD SAY THE TRAIN IS RESTING

One could say the train is resting when it's stopped
in the middle of the tracks, the passengers waiting
for the lulling sentiment of forward motion,
a love song woven into the wheels. *I love you,*

I love you, I love you, woven into the wheels.
That's the letter to the world she wrote.
The frosted lampshade dials down its output, then
emits a dreamy glow. To my left, a man is wearing

a suit: coat, pants, and tie. Anything I have on
makes me one of any number of hopeful
feminine heroines. I wrote a letter to the world.
The swan is not only singing but also playing

a harp. A true swan song. There's a humming
circle of feathers at its feet. In the dining car—
for luck—pinched salt is pressed tightly
between two fingers, then tossed over one shoulder.

Good luck with that. When I stand up,
the suit folds his flower hands and closes his eyes.
"Don't forget," he says, "all the spoils belong to me."
At that, the plastic raft at the center of the sea

slides back behind a blast of wind. The wildfire
makes the sunset blush. The seven people in the
sleeping car, each in a separate berth, hold their
collective breath. The story of obstacles overcome

is being recorded with the economy of an index
card. In the window's artificial eye, a perfect edge
and a battered edge are battling for their lives.

THE SCHOOL OF KNOWLEDGE

On the first day, light; on the second, water,
then the third, fourth, fifth, sixth, etcetera,
until you come to the lesson-centered day
you see the Milky Way as the downy drink

of morning. You're ever aware of the shared
terror of the shy kids souring the air
in the classroom. The globe spins daily
as you climb out of your asphalt and gravel

cereal. From seven to eight, boredom leaves
crumbs on the table, a hand wipes them away.
Quiet dies. Mouse eyes in a house-face.
The door swings open—a zero rolls out.

An inner voice says, Get yourself to a place
where you can see something other
than a spring spiraling up to infinity and you
caught in a cage, locked between

two rows of metal teeth, your head on a bed,
your last lover's long hair a smothering
blanket over you. Outside, Iceland moss
on a headstone serves as a token of loss.

Mother gone, father nonexistent. The plastic
ghost of an O settles itself in your long bones.
Goodnight love. Goodnight cost of living.
Goodbye. I close your eyes. I close my eyes.

SPEAKING OF THE FUTURE, HAMLET

is saying, someday this day will be over.
A moon will presumably still be above:
a bone quiet, an inflatable in the scene

—the cool blue swimming pool
it finds itself in. And I will want to be.
My mother, the Queen, will want only

my father, the King. All will be want
& get. And I will be me. And O, O,
Ophelia—will be the essence of love.

The love of a sister. Or, the love of the
brother. Compassion. Forgiveness.

All will be want & get. We will all be
together, on stage & in dress, reciting
our lines: "What a fine day. What a

wonderful way. To be." No sirens. Fifty
stars, a cloud. A drawing of an all-night
sky. We'll be there. You as you. And I.

ONCE UPON A TIME

"That's all," she said, "then, it's over."
What did she know?
She was a ghostlike apparitional sensory
effect chattering in my ear
about matters relevant only to me—

like a therapist in a chair going on and on
about last week's conundrum while you
lie there, suspended in air: a levitation
illusion, a pet shop sketch. For years
I'd said yes, but stopped before finishing

defining what yes meant. Today, I said yes,
I will say no. She nodded her head
in agreement. Instantly, in front of me,
a man. His hand raised. I admit I was afraid
of the final cut across my mouth, my lips,

flower petals folding in at the edge.
"Close your eyes," she said. I did. I saw
the room I'd hidden in. The single window
through which I used to look out
at a moon that made the cold night appear

as quaint as the pink feathery air
after fireworks that drifted slowly over
Tetris-tile blankets laid out on a beach
where the jigsaw-interlock of sand grains
mocked the ordinary imperfections inherent

in any life. The deaths past and present
in ashes, each discrete moment
a memory palace waiting to be built
alongside a suspended high-wire antenna
set to receive the unending message: this is
what is meant by your one and only life.

NOTES

The book's title, *A Film in Which I Play Everyone*, was inspired by a quote by David Bowie, "I'm looking for backing for an unauthorized autobiography that I am writing. Hopefully, this will sell in such huge numbers that I will be able to sue myself for an extraordinary amount of money and finance the film version in which I will play everybody." This was Bowie's response to a fan question from someone identified as Angst, who asked, "Any movie roles in the near future?" "David Bowie 50th Birthday Live Chat Transcription on AOL—8/1/97."

"Our Evening Is Over Us," which takes its title from a phrase in Gerard Manley Hopkins's "Spelt from Sibyl's Leaves," is for Paul Tran.

"The Key," which takes "a polar bear OUI" from a translation by Mary Jo Bang and Yuki Tanaka of the poem "MIROIR DE MIROIR : MIRRORED-MIRROR" by Shuzo Takiguchi, is for Yuki Tanaka.

"What Would I Have Been" is for Nick Flynn.

"How will it feel months from now" is for Cass Donnish.

"Elegy for Two" is in memory of Michael Donner Van Hook and Marni Ludwig.

"Reign of Terror" was inspired by Olympe de Gouges, feminist essayist and playwright, who was guillotined on November 3, 1793, at the Place de la Révolution for having written, among other things, the *Declaration of the Rights of Woman and of the Female Citizen*.

In "Some Identical Twin Sister, One Step Ahead," Rimbaud is paraphrased; what he said in his May 15, 1871, letter to Paul Demeny was, "Je dis qu'il faut être voyant, se faire voyant." (I'm saying one has to be a seer, to make oneself a seer.)

The quote in the first part of "Four Boxes of Everything" is from *Hamlet*, act 3, scene 1; in the second part, I believe the Dickinson is a paraphrase of something she said in a letter but I'm unable to locate the source.

The quote in "A Set Sketched by Light and Sound," is from Charles Lamb's essay, "Imperfect Sympathies."

The quote in "The shorthand method" is a translation of the prose introduction to the first sonnet of *Vita Nuova* by Dante Alighieri where Dante describes the moment when he is nine years old and first sees Beatrice.

"The hour of lead" in "Before the absolute perfection dying achieves" is from Dickinson's "After great pain a formal feeling comes" (#372).

The complete title of the book from which the quote in "The Echo" is taken is *The Empire of Russia: From the Remotest Periods to the Present Time*, first published in 1877.

In "Hanging the Curtain," "Will you, won't you join the dance?" comes from Lewis Carroll's *Alice's Adventures in Wonderland*.

The Marsden Hartley quote in "The Assumption" is taken from the Saint Louis Art Museum's online note that accompanies the image of the painting *Smelt Brook Falls*, oil on board, 1937.

The quote in "In This One World," is a paraphrase translation of Canto V, 107 in Dante's *Inferno* where Francesca says, "Caina attende chi a vita ci spense." (Caina waits for the one who snuffed out our lives.)

In "Staying Is a Form of Haunting," "The Dead" refers to the short story by James Joyce.

The quote in "Far from Here" is from Aeschylus's *Prometheus Bound*; I cannot locate the translation, so, unfortunately, cannot credit the translator.

In "Nothing Compares to Daphne in Green," "a Cerulean sky. *&*c. *&*c." comes from Thomas de Quincey's *The Confessions of an English Opium-Eater*; quoting lines from Wordsworth's "The Excursion," de Quincey breaks off at "Their station a cerulean sky" and adds "*&*c. *&*c."

In "The Doctor's Monster Is Drowning," "the core and substance of it untouched" comes from Mary Shelley's introduction to the 1831 edition of *Frankenstein; or, The Modern Prometheus*; the Virgil quote is a translation of "Trahit sua quemque voluptas" (Eclogues II, 65); "The watch-dogs bark! Bow-wow!" comes from *The Tempest*, act 1, scene 2.

"Mistress Mary, Quite" is an ekphrastic response to the painting *Mary, Mary Quite Contrary*, Maxfield Parrish, 1921.

ACKNOWLEDGMENTS

Thanks to the editors of the magazines and anthologies where the following poems appeared, sometimes in earlier versions:

The Academy of American Poets' *Poem-a-Day*: "A Miniature";

Action, Spectacle: "The Crowd Closes In," "I raised my wrist to my face," "The Doctor's Monster Is Drowning," and "I could have been better";

The American Poetry Review: "Here We All Are with Daphne," "Reign of Terror," "The Key," "Hotel Incognito," and "Once Upon a Time";

Australian Book Review: "The Experience of Being Outside";

Bat City Review: "This is me when I was busy with my needle," "Think of Jane and the Regency Era," "Before the absolute perfection dying achieves," "What I'm covering over" "Sometimes I Come to and Wonder," and "Hanging the Curtain";

The Brooklyn Rail: "The Trip," "From the Edge," and "On the Nature of Hardwiring";

Conjunctions: "Four Boxes of Everything" and "Mistress Mary, Quite";

jubilat: "The Therapist," "Far from Here," "The Actual Occurrences," and "Eyes Open, I Process the Data";

LIBER: A Feminist Review: "The Assumption";

LIT Magazine: "Nothing Compares to Daphne in Green" and "Part of a Larger Picture";

Mississippi Review: "Green Earth";

The New York Review of Books: "The Problem of the Present";

The New Yorker: "From Another Approach" and "The Bread, the Butter, the Orange Marmalade";

Ploughshares: "The School of Knowledge;

The Spectacle: "Some Identical Twin Sister, One Step Ahead";

Subtropics: "When I Was an Inanimate Object," "Elegy for Two," "What Would I Have Been," "The Fable of a Fabric Woven with Resistance," and "Our Evening Is Over Us";

Vallum: "Like Someone Asleep in a Cinema" and "I Am Already This Far";

Virginia Quarterly Review: "The War," "The Dead of Winter," "In the Movie of My Unraveling Mind," "This is what you are, the self says to the self," "Today you're the still photographer," and "A Starting Point";

"How will it feel months from now" and "Speaking of the future, Hamlet" were originally published with the Shelter in Poems initiative on poets.org, an online publication of the Academy of American Poets;

"Like Someone Asleep in a Cinema" was included in *The Pushcart Prize XLIII: Best of the Small Presses* (2019 edition);

"One Could Say the Train Is Resting" was included in *The Eloquent Poem: 128 Contemporary Poems and Their Making*, ed. Elise Paschen, Persea Press, 2019;

"On the Factory Floor" [as "A Woman Overheard Speaking"] was included in *The Poetry of Capital: Voices from Twenty-First-Century America*, ed. Benjamin S. Grossberg and Clare Rossini, University of Wisconsin Press, 2021;

"A Set Sketched by Light and Sound" was included in *I Know What's Best for You: Stories on Reproductive Freedom*, ed. Shelly Oria, McSweeney's, 2022;

"Children Were Erasing Their Faces" was included in *The Night's Magician: Poems about the Moon*, ed. Philip C. Kolin and Sue Brannan Walker, Negative Capability Press, 2018;

The most profound thanks to Joni Wallace, without whose encouragement and insight these poems would not be keeping each other company between the covers of this book. Thanks to Timothy Donnelly for his incisive comments on the poems and for helping to choreograph the manuscript. Thanks to David Schuman and Jennifer Kronovet for their careful reading of the manuscript and their helpful comments. To these friends and to the others unnamed, thank you for the brightest days and loveliest nights. And an entire kingdom of gratitude to Bill Clegg, Jeff Shotts, and everyone at Graywolf Press who worked to make this book this book.

Mary Jo Bang is the author of eight previous books of poems—including *A Doll for Throwing*, *The Last Two Seconds*, *The Bride of E*, and *Elegy*, which received the National Book Critics Circle Award. She has published translations of Dante Alighieri's *Inferno*, illustrated by Henrik Drescher, and *Purgatorio*, as well as *Colonies of Paradise*, poems by the German poet and novelist Matthias Göritz. She has received a Hodder Fellowship, a Guggenheim Fellowship, and a Berlin Prize Fellowship. She is a professor of English at Washington University in St. Louis where she teaches creative writing.

The text of *A Film in Which I Play Everyone* is set in Libre Baskerville. Book design and composition by Bookmobile Design & Digital Publisher Services, Minneapolis, Minnesota. Manufactured by Friesens on acid-free, 100 percent postconsumer wastepaper.